cloverleaf books™

Fall's Here!

S0-AXO-612

# Fall Harvests

## Bringing in Food

Martha E. H. Rustad

illustrated by Amanda Enright

MAIN LIBRARY
Champaign Public Library
200 West Green Street
Champaign, Illinois 61820-5193

M MILLBROOK PRESS · MINNEAPOLIS

In honor of my grandparents, who harvested many crops from the North Dakota soil
—M.E.H.R.

Text and illustrations copyright © 2012 by Lerner Publishing Group, Inc.

All rights reserved. International copyright secured. No part of this book may be reproduced, stored in a retrieval system, or transmitted in any form or by any means—electronic, mechanical, photocopying, recording, or otherwise—without the prior written permission of Lerner Publishing Group, Inc., except for the inclusion of brief quotations in an acknowledged review.

Millbrook Press
A division of Lerner Publishing Group, Inc.
241 First Avenue North
Minneapolis, MN 55401 U.S.A.

Website address: www.lernerbooks.com

Main body text set in Slappy Inline 18/28.
Typeface provided by T26.

Library of Congress Cataloging-in-Publication Data

Rustad, Martha E. H. (Martha Elizabeth Hillman), 1975–
    Fall harvests : bringing in food / by Martha E. H.
  Rustad ; illustrated by Amanda Enright.
       p.    cm. — (Cloverleaf books. Fall's here!)
    Includes index.
    ISBN 978–0–7613–5067–5 (lib. bdg. : alk. paper)
    1. Harvesting—Juvenile literature. I. Enright, Amanda,
  ill.  II. Title.
  SB129.R925  2012
  631.5'5—dc22                          2010053467

Manufactured in the United States of America
1 – BP – 7/15/11

# TABLE OF CONTENTS

Yum! I help my dad make applesauce. We eat pecan pie and pumpkin bread every Thanksgiving.

4

Some of my favorite **foods** are **harvested in the fall.**

In fall, apples, pecans, and pumpkins are all ripe, ready to eat.

But last spring, they all started off small.

# Chapter Two

# Growing Food

## Spring *is for* planting.

In spring, farmers plant seeds to grow food for people and animals.

CORN

Tiny sprouts push out of the dirt. They will grow into pumpkins, turnips, potatoes, and corn. In orchards, apple and pecan trees blossom in the spring.

Pumpkins

Potatoes

Farmers plant seeds far apart. Plants need lots of room to grow. By fall, the plants will fill in the spaces.

# Summer is for growing.

**Leaves** turn sunlight into food for growing plants.

**Roots** gather water for thirsty plants.

8

The green color inside leaves is called chlorophyll. Chlorophyll makes food for plants.

**Slowly, plants change and grow.**

**Weeds and bugs** can hurt growing plants. Weeds crowd out growing crops. Bugs eat growing leaves.

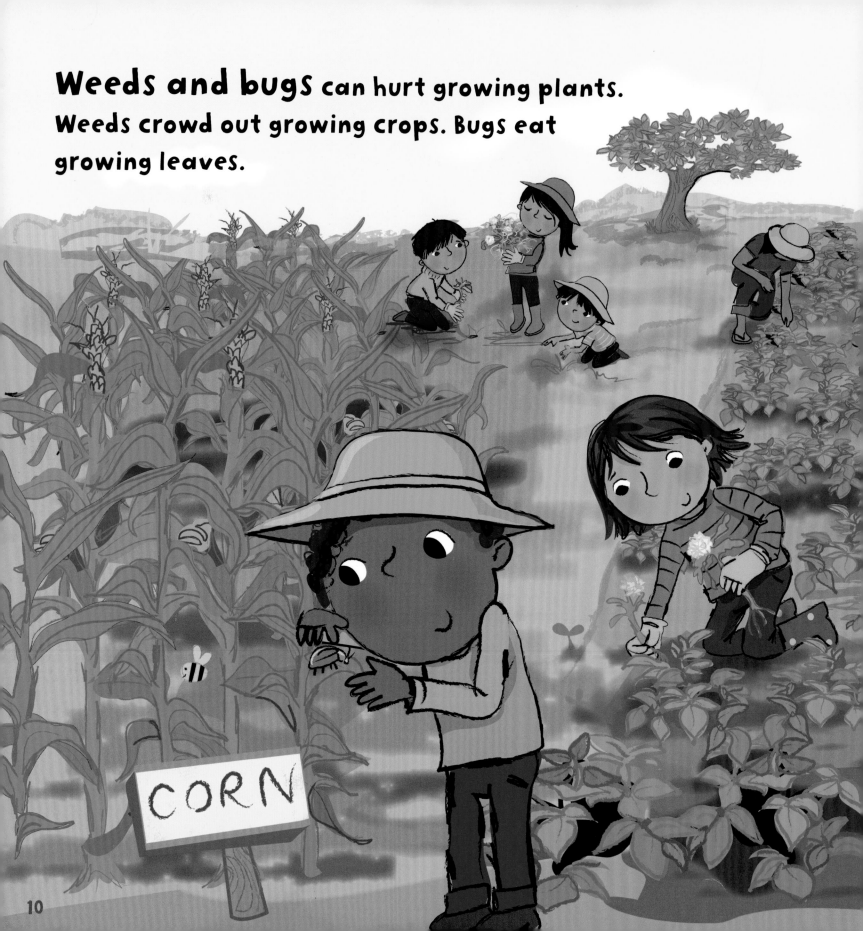

CORN

Farmers and gardeners work hard to stop weeds and bugs.

Pumpkins

Potatoes

People pull weeds with tools, machines, and their hands. Some gardeners pick bugs off by hand too.

11

# Chapter Three

# Harvesting Food

**Fall** is for **harvesting.**

Plants stop growing in the cool fall weather.

Crops are ripe and ready for harvest. People harvest food using their hands or machines.

Some farmers also plant grain seeds in fall. These grains grow a little in fall. They stop growing in winter. They start growing again in spring. They are ripe in early summer.

Farmers harvest fruit from orchard trees in fall. People pick ripe apples and peaches by hand.

Ripe pecans fall from pecan trees. Farmers sometimes use machines to shake pecans from trees.

Farmers know when apples and peaches are ready to be picked. Ripe fruit is easy to pull off the tree.

15

# Chapter Four

# Harvest Festivals

People around the world have **festivals in fall.** The festivals are parties to celebrate all the food harvested that year.

In Korea, people have the Harvest Moon Festival. They eat rice cakes and play games.

At the Yam Festival in Ghana, people laugh and dance.

They eat yams, walk in parades, and make music.

In North America, Thanksgiving is a time for **family**. Families eat big meals, watch parades, and play sports.

In fall, the earth gets ready to rest.
Farmers and gardeners get ready to rest too.

I am thankful for the **fall harvest**. What is your favorite fall food?

# Make a Corn Husk Friend

Save the corn husks you peel away from corn. Now you can make a little friend!

**What You Need:**
dried corn husks (dry your own or buy at a craft store), about 6 per friend
wide, shallow container of water
towel
heavy string or yarn
scissors
decorative items (construction paper, glue, markers, buttons, yarn, etc.)

What You Do:

1) Soak the dried corn husks in the water for about an hour.

2) Take four husks and lay them on a towel, pointed sides up.
   Tie them together at the bottom.

3) Fold down two of these husks on each side. Tie a string about 1" (2.5 cm)
   from the top to make the head.

4) Roll a new husk tightly, and tie each end with a string. Stick this rolled husk
   in between the husks hanging down below the neck. This makes the arms.
   Tie a string below the arms to make the waist.

5) To make shoulders, wrap another husk diagonally across the chest and back.
   Wrap a second husk across the other side of the chest and back. Tie another
   string around the waist to hold these in place.

6) To make legs, divide the husks hanging
   down. Tie at the knees and ankles. To
   make a dress, leave the husks untied.

7) Decorate your corn husk friend.

For step-by-step pictures on making
a corn husk friend, check out:
http://www.teachersfirst.com/summer/cornhusk.htm.

# GLOSSARY

**blossom:** when flowers grow on a tree or a bush

**celebrate:** to do something fun on a special day, such as have a party

**chlorophyll:** a substance inside leaves that makes them green and helps make food for plants

**crops:** plants that are usually grown for food

**festivals:** big parties

**harvested:** picked. Crops are harvested when they are ready to be eaten.

**pecan:** a nut that grows on trees

**ripe:** ready to be picked and eaten

**root:** a part of a plant that grows underground. Roots soak up water and bring it to the stem.

**sprout:** a small, young plant

## BOOKS

Harris, Nicholas. *A Year at a Farm.* Minneapolis: Millbrook Press, 2009.

Head, Honor. *Harvest Festivals around the World.* New York: PowerKids Press, 2009.

Rotner, Shelley. *Senses on the Farm.* Minneapolis: Millbrook Press, 2009.

## WEBSITES

**Giant Pumpkin**
http://www.youtube.com/watch?v=oIzs2LShElc&feature=fvw
Watch a video of how a farmer grows a giant pumpkin.

**How a Pumpkin Grows**
http://www.kizclub.com/Topics/food/pumpkin.pdf
Print out and color cards that show how a pumpkin grows. You can mix the cards and then try to put them in the right order.

**Kids' Zone: Agriculture in the Classroom**
http://www.agclassroom.org/kids/index.htm
Play games and learn more about farming at this website.